Honey Bee

Jane Hileman   Katie Axt

I am a honey bee.
I live with lots of bees.

This is our hive.

I'm one of the bees that goes out to get food. Lots of us go out to get food.

Some bees don't go out.
They have to be at the hive.

Can you see my wings?
I have four wings.

I can fly fast. I fly out to look for food.

We get our food from flowers.

Let's go get some. Where are the flowers we like?

Can you see my eyes?
I have five eyes.

I can see flowers from up here.
I see them with my two big eyes.

Let's go home and get lots of bees.

They'll come here, too.

Here they come.

Let's see if these flowers are good.

You have a nose.
You smell with your nose.

I don't have a nose. I smell with these.
Is this a good flower?

You have a tongue.
You taste with your tongue.

I taste with my six feet.
Is this a good flower?

Yes! This is a good flower.

I'll take out the straw I have inside me.

I drink juice from the flower.
I drink juice from many flowers.

Now I'll go to the hive and give the juice to a bee in the hive.

Here I come.

The bees in the hive will make the juice into honey. Food for all!

Honey Bees

Honey Bee is a worker bee. All worker bees are female. Each hive has thousands of worker bees. When Honey Bee was young, she fed the baby bees in the hive. As she grew older, she helped make nectar into honey. When she was strong enough and old enough, she began to go out into the world to find flowers and bring nectar back to the hive. Honey Bee only lived about five weeks. Just the right life for a bee.

I can use the first letter sound to match the word to the picture.

honey

feet

bee

flower

nose

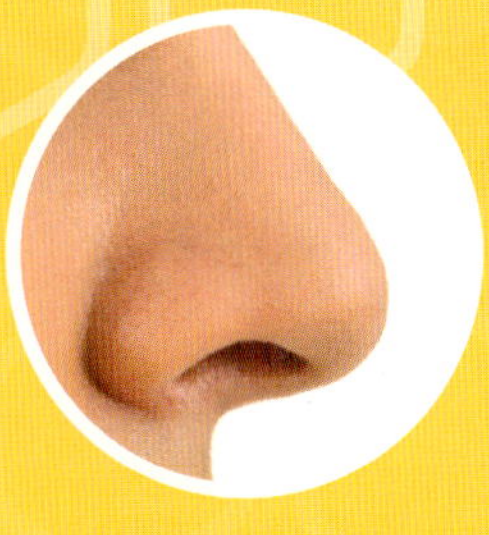

Power Words

How many can you read?

1G

a	be	go	live	that	we
all	big	have	look	the	where
am	can	here	lots	they	will
and	come	I	my	this	with
are	for	is	of	to	yes
at	get	like	see	up	you

2G

don't	goes	into	many	six	they'll
five	good	if	now	some	too
four	home	inside	one	take	two
from	I'll	let's	our	them	your
give	I'm	make	out	these